MONEY MATTERS FOR THERAPISTS

a financial guide for self-employed therapists and counsellors

Robert Tyler

Worth Publishing

www.worthpublishing.com

First published by Worth Publishing Ltd., 2003
6 Lauderdale Parade, London W9 1LU
www.worthpublishing.com

ISBN 1-903269-07-5

Printed and bound in Great Britain by Bath Press, Bath, UK

Cover and text design by Caroline Harper

© Worth Publishing 2003

CONTENTS

INTRODUCTION

The purpose of this book is to deal with all the main financial issues for therapists and counsellors in one reference guide. In writing it, I am drawing on many years financial experience; in addition, I am married to a therapist, and have friends who practice as therapists and counsellors, so I have learnt a lot about their working life! As far as my partner and I are aware, until now, there has been no book published about the financial aspects of being a therapist or counsellor. Perhaps this is because, for many in these professions, money is not the principle focus of attention - despite the reasonable and almost universal interest in earning more.

Although much of this book is relevant to anyone who is self-employed, great care has been taken here to relate **Money Matters** to the practical considerations experienced by therapists and counsellors in their everyday life. Of course there will be people who merit special consideration - single parents with young children, or the disabled, for example - to whom additional tax related benefits will apply; these matters are not covered here as they vary according to individual circumstances. Inevitably, too, the current (May 2003) tax rules will change over time and new ones be brought in; but the basic principles will undoubtedly remain the same.

I thought it sensible to start with a little 'self-exploration'. Hence the first section asks you to consider what financial rewards you are seeking, and offers some practical ideas on how to move toward your objective.

And from conversations I have had with therapists and counsellors, it is clear that many of you are not aware of the expenses you can claim to help offset (reduce) your tax bill each year. I hope, therefore, for the modest cost of this book (which is, after all, tax deductible!) hard-working therapists and counsellors throughout the UK will keep hundreds, if not thousands, more pounds for themselves.

Robert Tyler
London, June 2003

PLANNING YOUR PRACTICE

1. How much money do you want to earn?

Well, it's a fairly fundamental point. The question of how much money you would like to earn is also linked to how much time you wish to devote to your practice. This is particularly true if you are engaged on other projects (such as writing a book), or are employed part-time, or perhaps have other commitments, such as growing children or dependant relatives.

You can ask yourself these two fundamental questions any time, and changes can be made to your existing practice over time to accord with new priorities or wishes. It may be that you want to cut down your practice client numbers, to release time to do some research work, take up a tutor position at a further education college, or simply have a break! Alternatively, you may think that you are not making enough money for the effort you are already putting in, and want to correct that. In any case, it is helpful to bring the question **"How much money do I want to earn?"** to mind regularly.

Time is definitely money! So please, **decide the annual income you want now**, and I will show you how to plan to achieve this in subsections 2 and 3 that follow.

2. How can I achieve the income I want?

If you are not obtaining the income objective you have now decided upon, there are three ways to move towards it:

- **Put up your hourly fee rates**
- **Increase the hours you work**
- **Reduce the costs of your practice**

- and of course you can do one, two or all three of these things. The most effective action for most people will be to **increase fees** and **reduce costs**.

EXAMPLE

Nadia is a therapist with two small children, who has to employ a childminder for 15 hours a week at a cost of £75. She works 25 client hours a week, including a visit to an agency to see two clients; the agency is an hour's drive away. Her average hourly rate is £22. She uses a consulting room above a local health food shop, which costs her £4 per hour. Her supervisor lives half an hour away. Although Nadia earns £550 per week in fees, her expenses are £260 per week, leaving her £290 before tax and benefits. She is exhausted, her car needs a major service and she has little savings.

Nadia decided, after taking advice from a friend, to tell her clients that her fees would increase to an average hourly rate of £27 per hour, and to try to negotiate with the agency to increase her fee to £35 per hour. In total, Nadia lost seven clients over a six month period, including the agency clients. This meant her weekly income was £486; but she was able to reduce her weekly expenses on room-hire, childcare and travel by £100 per week (total expenses £160 per week), leaving her £326 per week before tax and benefits. She is £36 per week better off and has reduced her working hours by nine (7 client hours and two hours of journey time).

Once you have adjusted your current programme of work along such lines as you think sensible in relation to cost and effort, you can then consider how to achieve your ideal income. If you are starting a new practice, then what follows is essential information to help you plan your financial reward.

I will use the titles **therapist** and **counsellor** throughout, but this will also include people who practice as supervisors and trainers in these fields.

3. How to work out how much to charge and how long to work

I recognise that client fees, expenses, and available working hours all vary hugely according to the individual therapist's or counsellor's circumstances. I also recognise that it is very difficult to plan precisely how many hours you will work in any given year, as usually the number of clients who may start or end therapy or counselling with you is unpredictable. Further, some therapists like to offer sliding-scale fees to a proportion of clients who may be less able to afford the standard fee than others; this can also lead to complexity in ensuring you have enough income to meet your own needs.

There is a way to overcome all these problems.

On page 5 overleaf I have set up a chart entitled - **Therapists and Counsellors - Plot your ideal income**. The chart shows a weekly income. To convert this to an annual income, you need to multiply the amount by the number of weeks you intend to work - I have assumed 48 weeks.

Weekly fee income is the product of the number of hours worked multiplied by the hourly charge rate. The chart overleaf shows a number of weekly target earnings curves (from £200 to £800 - but you could add different ones). You can stop anywhere on the curve by travelling along the bottom axis of *number of hours worked a week*, or by travelling up the side axis of *rate charged per hour*. Wherever you stop on the curve, you will achieve your ideal income by looking at how many hours you need and the resultant rate per hour.

I have also added a curve to show at what point you must register for

VAT. The chart gives four simple examples:

- 10 hours at £20 per hour = £200 per week
- 15 hours at £25 per hour = £375 per week
- 20 hours at £30 per hour = £600 per week
- 25 hours at £32 per hour = £800 per week

More importantly, you can pick either

> ■ **your charge rate (standard fee) and desired income and see how many hours you need to work;**

or,

> ■ **the hours you want to work and the desired income, and work out what rate you must charge.**

When you pick the **hours worked** figure, it is important to err on the cautious side (pick a lower figure than you actually currently do or would do), to allow for the client uncertainties mentioned above. You can plot other desired incomes curves yourself using the same chart.

EXAMPLE
David, a counsellor, has decided he wants to earn £600 per week by charging £30 per hour and working 20 hours per week.

Now we have to consider David's expenses, since these will have to be deducted from the income figure he has picked.

Expenses incurred everyday by therapists and counsellors are normally what are technically called **variable costs**; that means they occur only if you are working, and **do not** occur if you are **not** working. These are - room hire, supervision, and travel, and can easily be expressed as hourly costs.

(There will be times you have to cancel a session unexpectedly (if you are ill, for example) when you will still incur room-hire charges. You might want to slightly increase your calculated average hourly cost to allow for this factor).

Step 2: Stop anywhere along the curve when the rate per hour or the hours worked suits you

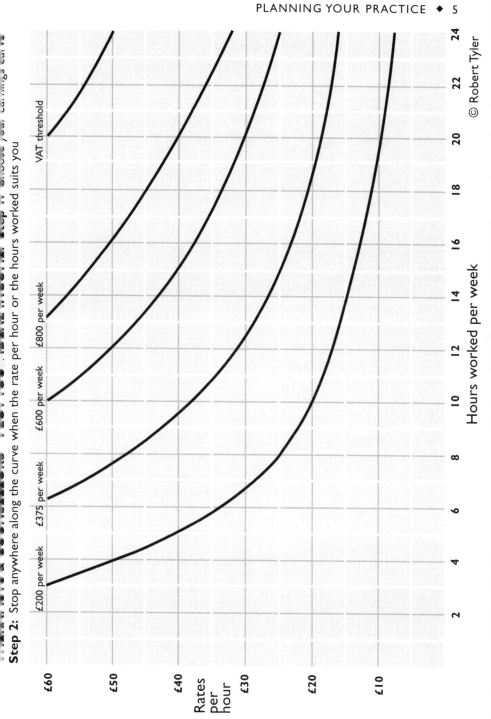

© Robert Tyler

David's **everyday variable** *costs are:*
- *Room Hire*   *£5 per hour*
- *Supervision*   *£1.50 per hour (£60 per fortnight)*
- *Travel*   *£2 per hour (£40 per week)*

Total   **£8.50 per hour**

Based on his chosen working week of 20 hours.

There are, however, other costs incurred by therapists and counsellors which are not related necessarily to hourly work. Such costs might typically be: professional membership, essential continuing professional development (which may spread over a year), insurance, advertising and stationery costs. These costs are known as **fixed costs**, because they **do not vary** according to the number of hours of work you do. They need to be added together for the year, and then divided by the hours worked to get an hourly rate.

David's annual **fixed** *costs are:*
- *Professional membership*   *£100*
- *CPD Training*   *240*
- *Fees*   *80*
- *Insurance*   *110*
- *Phone*   *370*
- *Advertising on Internet*   *380*
- *Stationery*   *160*

Total   **£1,440**

David's ideal working week is 20 hours, and he wants 4 weeks off a year; so in total, he works 960 hours a year.

£1,440 divided by 960 is £1.50 per hour.
Adding the everyday and annual costs together, David's expenses
*amount to £10 per hour (£8.50 **variable costs** as above, + £1.50 for*
*other **fixed** costs).*

Once you know your hourly costs, you can then revisit your income
plan and insert this figure. This will clearly considerably reduce your
planned income.

David's ideal income of £600 per week has now been reduced by his
costs, which are £10 per hour for his chosen 20 hour, ie £200 per week.
He is thus left with £400 per week income and must now modify his
plan to get back to £600 per week net income.

In order to get back to your desired income there are three options for
you (assuming you have already made whatever cost savings you can):

1. Increase the hourly charge rate by the amount your expenses cost per hour
David could increase his standard fee by £10 per hour to £40 per hour,
and thus maintain his target income. £40 per hour multiplied by 20
hours = £800 per week, less £200 per week costs, brings David back to
£600 per week.

2. Work more hours in the week.
Each extra hour worked, however, brings with it extra hourly costs, so
the increase in hours may work out more than first thought.

David is concerned that to increase fees to £40 per hour would not be
fair or acceptable to his clients, so he wants to look at extending his
hours to achieve his target income of £600 per week. David needs an
extra £200 per week. Although he will charge £30 per hour for each
extra hour worked, he will also pay £8.50 per hour in variable costs
(room hire, more supervision and travel), thus leaving him with £21.50

per hour clear. David divided the £200 he needed extra by the hourly income rate of £21.50 and found that he needed to work 10 hours more each week - 30 hours in total to obtain his target income of £600 per week. (Note: David's fixed annual costs of membership subscription, CPD training, advertising, etcetera have already been paid for in the 20 basic hours he wants to work).

3. A third option is to apply both option 1 and option 2; charge more and work longer.

A modest increase in fee rate will have a disproportionately helpful effect on the number of hours that need to be worked.

David has decided that his income objective is sacrosanct. He feels he can increase his fee to £35 per hour, and wants to see what effect this has on the hours he must do. He is charging an extra £5 per hour for 20 hours so this will give him an extra £100 per week of the £200 per week he needs. The remaining £100 will have to come from extra hours. Each hour will cost David £8.50 in variable cost, but this will now be deducted from £35. This leaves a net income of £26.50 for each extra hour worked. As David has to find an extra £100 he need only work an extra 4 hours a week (£100 divided by £26.50).

David now works out his annual budget:

■ Income:
  1152 hours (48 weeks x 24) at £35 per hour = £40,320
Less:
  ■ Expenses:
  Variable (1152hours x £8.50 per hour) = £9,792
  Annual = £1,440

  ■ Total expenses: £11,232

  Net Income *(£606 for each of 48 working weeks)* **£29,088**

Sliding scale fees for clients

Now that the income target has been achieved and all expenses taken care of, it is possible to calculate the sliding scale fees you may wish to offer other clients. Providing you select a fee that **slightly exceeds your variable costs per hour** as a starting point on your scale, there is no danger of you affecting your target income.

David wishes to offer a further two or three hours counselling on a sliding-scale. His variable costs are £8.50 per hour, so he decides to commence his scale at £10 per hour.

All the information above applies irrespective of whether you work part-time as a therapist or counsellor, or full-time.

Although playing with average figures can be playing with fire, there is, for therapists and counsellors, a very broad correlation between the fee charged per hour and the net annual income you can achieve. **Your annual income will work out at not less than 1,000 times your hourly fee for a 30 hour working week.** So if you charge £35 per hour and work thirty hours a week for 48 weeks, your net income should be at least £35,000 a year.

Thirty hours a week is a lot for most therapists and counsellors. Increasing your hourly rate would cut down the hours needed to achieve a fair professional living. It is interesting that the average hourly rate in the UK for therapists and counsellors is less than half that in the USA. It is also worth noting that therapists' and counsellors' hourly rate is about a fifth that now charged now by accountants and solicitors - fellow professionals.

Section B
KEY FINANCIAL ISSUES

1. Are you self - employed?

This is a very important question, currently the subject of much interest to the Inland Revenue.

A therapist or counsellor can either be:
- an employee
- self-employed
- both

An employee is someone who is on the payroll of, or who works solely for, an employer, such as social services or the NHS. *Note*: if your sole employer accepts an invoice from you for fees, you may still be considered as an employee by the Inland Revenue. This would be the case if all your work came from a single agency.

Someone who is **self-employed** only issues bills to clients for fees, usually to members of the general public (i.e. clients) or to various institutions/companies.

If you can answer YES to the following questions you are self-employed:

- Do you have the final say in how your practice is run?
- Do you risk your own money when operating your practice?
- Are you responsible for meeting losses as well as taking profits?
- Do you provide the main items of equipment you need to do your job?

- Are you free to hire people if you need them?
- Do you have to correct unsatisfactory work in your own time and at your own expense?

A therapist or counsellor can also be both employed and self-employed. You might, for example, be a tutor on a university course and on their payroll, with tax deducted by your employer, and you might also be in private practice. In these circumstances, it is **vitally important that you keep separate records for your private practice**. Your final tax return will show both activities accounted for separately. (Section C provides a more detailed consideration of what this means in practice).

If you are solely an employee, you cannot normally deduct operating expenses from your income before tax; whereas if you are self-employed, you can (see Section D). The vast majority of therapists and counsellors are either self-employed, or both. This book assumes that you are self-employed. **Being self-employed means you are running a business** - we will call it the TC business.

If you are just about to start a self-employed business as a therapist or counsellor for the first time, you must tell the Inland Revenue within **three months** of issuing your first fees invoice.

As a self-employed businessperson, a therapist or counsellor can chose what year-end date the business shall have to prepare its annual accounts. In my view it is better to choose the tax year as your business year-end (i.e. April 5th). This is because it is much simpler to prepare figures (you avoid having to split your year into two to suit the tax year). **You will have to pay tax twice in the year** (see Section F - Income Tax).

If I am running a business, should I start a Company?
Occasionally people enquire if it is sensible to run a TC business as a Limited Company. A Limited Company is a legal trading entity whose

liability to losses is limited (generally speaking) to the amount of money invested by you in the business. The short answer to the question, **"Should I start a Company?"** is probably no, because, in most cases, creating a Company is an unnecessary complication for what is a straightforward personal tax issue.

For those of you who might wish to pursue this further, the key points are:

In favour of being a Limited Company:

■ If you already pay tax at the highest marginal rate of 40% you may save tax if you are *also* self-employed, by paying net profits made by your Limited Company out to yourself in dividends as a company shareholder.

The tax saving relies on currently low corporation tax rates for Limited Companies and low dividend tax rates, compared to 40%.

The tax paid by individuals on dividends up to £30,500 is currently 10% (2003/4), if this is the only income. Over £30,500, the dividend tax rate is 32.5%.

Against being a Limited Company:

■ Because of the complexities of this method of trading, you will need to use an accountant who will charge a fee

■ You depend on the government not changing a range of tax rates, which is risky, and frankly, unlikely.

■ Your self-employed finances will become public property from the information you have to file each year at Companies House.

■ You will have additional administrative burdens.

In reality, most therapists and counsellors will work as self-employed people and prepare accounts once a year. Your accounts will show income and expenses, and are used to calculate…TAX.

2. What being a business means

Everyone who works between the age of 18-60 (women) and 18-65 (men) must pay income tax and/or national insurance contributions. National Insurance is, to all intents and purposes, another form of income tax. Everyone also has to submit a tax return each year, either -

■ **by the 30th September after the tax year (6th April to 5th April) if you want the Inland Revenue to calculate the tax you owe.**

or

■ **by 31st January the following year if you wish to calculate your own tax bill yourself.**

Nowadays, the Inland Revenue relies on self-assessment for tax, which means they trust you, but it also means that the responsibility for record-keeping is squarely on your shoulders. This is nothing to worry about, but it does underline the need for you to keep your papers in a safe place, and to keep information as up-to-date as possible.

Even if the terminology is unfamiliar, **being self-employed means you are a business**. There are advantages. Because, technically, you are a business, your expenditure can be deducted from your income before income tax is paid. There are also **business tax allowances**, and special rates of National Insurance which will apply to you.

Because you are a business, you also need to be aware of **Value Added Tax (VAT)**. You must register to be a VAT registered business **if your income exceeds or is expected to exceed £56,000 in one year**.

For small businesses, VAT is paid once a year. Once you are registered, you can claim back VAT charged to you on expense items, and you must charge VAT on your fee bills. **If you are not registered for VAT, you must deduct VAT from your expenses before you claim them against tax.**

Income tax or profits tax for self-employed people is calculated like this:

- **Sales/Income/Fees**
    Less
- **Allowable expenses**
    Equals
- **Income/Profit <u>before</u> tax calculations**

> Tax is not calculated on your income;
> it is calculated on your income
> **<u>after</u>** expenses have been deducted.

Allowable expenses are items which can legitimately be deducted from income before tax is calculated and paid (see section D). 'Legitimately' means expenses incurred wholly and exclusively for your business as a therapist or counsellor.

**The higher your income, the <u>more</u> tax you pay;
the higher your expenses, the <u>less</u> tax you pay.**

It is obviously essential to keep accurate and dated records of **income** and **expenditure**. Although this is best done on computer (use Microsoft Excel if you have it, or Appleworks), computer records on their own are not sufficient evidence for tax purposes. Paper records of fees charged and copies of expense bills and receipts need to be kept, and in date order on file. If there is no paper record, create your own record with the date and detail described. Always keep a note of what you pay into the bank and whom each individual item is from (see Section C – *Confidentiality*). When you issue a cheque, make a note of the person it is paid to and the reason for it (see Section C – Your minimum paperwork).

As self-employed business people, therapists and counsellors, must, by law, keep annual accounts records for **5 years after the last final date of filing your tax return**. This means if you filed using the 30th September deadline in 2002 you must keep these records up to 30th September 2007 (five years and six months), and if you filed using the 31st January 2003 deadline you must keep these records up to 31st January 2008 (five years and ten months).

Finally, it is very important (and also helpful to you) that you can **distinguish between your personal finances and records, and your business ones**. This point is often not fully appreciated, as my discussions with therapists testify. Many therapists and counsellors regularly confuse their business financial affairs with their personal ones. Ways of avoiding this easily are covered in the next section. If the Inland Revenue ever chooses you as a target for a full investigation (hopefully never!), this point about a proper separation of your business and private lives is the most important.

3. Do you need an accountant?

If you have a friend who is one, then he/she may be able or willing to help. Generally, however, it is not necessary to have an accountant unless you have difficulty understanding the concepts in this book, or if you frankly find figures too difficult or irritating to deal with.

There are accountants who have a great deal of experience in your field, who are very good and helpful. It is probably best to ask friends for recommendations since, like supervisors, it is best to be comfortable with the person who will handle your personal affairs.

Accountants will charge fees (which are tax deductible). Typically fees should be somewhere between £350 and £750 per annum plus VAT, subject to geographical area and the time they have to put in on your work. If you do wish to use, or already use, an accountant, you should be able to save fees if you present information to him or her using the record-keeping suggestions described in Section C (Your minimum paperwork).

Section C

HOW TO DO YOUR ACCOUNTS

I. The Bank

It is vital that your personal money affairs are separate from your therapy or counselling business affairs. The first and most important step is to establish a completely new and separate current (interest bearing) bank account for your business. We will call it - **TC business account**. You should also do this if you are already established. Although banks will give new businesses free banking for twelve or even eighteen months, you will eventually have to pay monthly fees to the bank. These fees are calculated on each transaction.

You will **pay in** all the client fees you receive, and any other money coming into the practice, into the **TC business account**. From this account, you will also **pay out** all expenses, including payments to yourself in the form of 'wages', (listed as 'drawings for self' in the analysis sheet on p. 25). These **'wages'** from the TC business account should be paid into your personal account. Your personal account should then pay for your personal needs. **You should not pay for your personal needs by using cheques drawn on your TC business account.** If you ignore this advice, it will cause you paperwork confusion, and questions may eventually be raised by the Tax Inspector as to which items are legitimate expenses for the business; you may lose his or her goodwill and even, in extreme circumstances, be fined.

If you anticipate that there will be sums in excess of £10,000 in the TC business account on a regular basis, it might also be sensible to set up a **TC business reserve account**. This pays higher interest, but allows you or the bank to move funds backwards and forwards to the TC business account whenever needed.

If you have an overdraft or borrowings/mortgages on your personal account, it may be better to open your TC business account at a different bank altogether. This is because most banks get you to sign to say that they can transfer *any* sum *any* time from *any* account of yours in surplus, to reduce *any* account of yours in deficit within that bank *and* its subsidiaries (it's all there in that small print!). This will include any *joint accounts* you may have, and your credit card/s. Clearly you would not wish your business account to be affected in this way; thus using an entirely separate bank is worth considering in this context. A bank like Alliance and Leicester currently has very low handling charges for small businesses such as those run by therapists and counsellors.

Because you are established and educated professionals, therapists and counsellors generally enjoy a high credit standing amongst lenders, and you ought to be well received wherever you go. Banks also provide free, straightforward accounting software and/or forms for TC businesses, which can be used as summary sheets for calculating your final profit. Just ask the business manager at any time.

Some banks, which also issue credit cards, will provide another credit card that you can use entirely for your business. This could be useful for any form of expense. In some cases, the credit card company can provide an annual summary of card use according to type of expense. MBNA bank is an example of a bank that does this, but there are others. Using the business credit card can also help ensure you keep your personal affairs and your TC business separate. If you have more than one card already, you could simply dedicate one to the business. Using one credit card for both private and business purposes is definitely *not* recommended, as it will cause a lot of record keeping complications. If you use any credit card for business, it is best to use a TC business account cheque to pay off the specific TC business expenses on that card, and use a personal cheque to pay off the personal expenses.

If you are going to use the computer for your business record-keeping, you might like to consider Internet banking for your business account. Apart from the advantage of obtaining immediate information, you can also access it from anywhere in the world.

2. Client fees - your income

Discussing money issues with your clients, existing or potential, can be challenging for both parties. It is really essential that financial issues are fully explained and dealt with clearly in the client contract at the inception of therapy or counselling, and that they therefore form a core part of the therapeutic frame. Equally, if work is undertaken for institutions or commercial organisations, you should be clear in the original contract about the terms of remuneration (hours and rates of pay) and the treatment of disbursements (expenses incurred by you solely in connection with this work and for which you intend to invoice). All invoices raised by you, whether for fees or disbursements, are considered as **sales** or **income**.

Confidentiality
The names of your private clients are confidential. You will therefore need to develop a code system for your paperwork, in relation to client fees, so that their names do not appear anywhere. The easiest way is to allocate each client a number or an initial, and keep a private record of to which client each code refers. Use these codes in your analysis book (*see below*) and on the actual invoice itself.

3. The minimum paperwork you need

You need to keep the following minimum records separately for each tax year.

- An analysis of what money has been **paid in** to the bank, and why
- An analysis of what money has been **paid out** of the bank, and why
- Both of these records can be made in **one analysis book** with lots of columns. (I find the Collins Cathedral Analysis Book Number 150/12.1 ideal for this purpose - and see pages 24 and 25 below)
- Keep your TC business account bank statements in a **statement file** (the bank will give you a free one)
- Retain **all** of your **chequebook stubs** and **paying in slips** to the bank in **one box file.**
- Finally you need **one lever arch file** with a central divider. At the front, place copies of **your fee invoices**, filed in date order; in the back, place all **your expense invoices** in **date of invoice order**.

This is all the paperwork you need. One analysis book, statement file, box file, lever arch file. All of these items are available from good stationers (and their cost is tax-deductible!). If you handle a lot of cash you may need to keep a separate record of this (see sub-section 4).

The analysis book contains the key information. This should be prepared along the lines of the two examples that follow. The first example is for amounts **paid in** to the bank, which you should list on **the left hand page**, and the second example is for amounts **paid out** of the bank, which you need to list on the **right hand page**.

It is important that expenses are analysed **excluding VAT**, even if you are not VAT registered, as you can only deduct expenses excluding VAT from income.

You will notice that the **paid in** example has a voucher number column. It is not necessary to number your fee invoices, but the date/s of the invoice/s must be inserted for cross-referencing to the lever arch file. When someone pays, you should make a note in the lever arch file that the invoice was paid, and the date.

For other payments into the bank, you should use the number printed on your paying-in slip as a voucher number.

The **paid out** page also has a voucher number column on it. This is for expenses type invoices. In the lever arch file each expense invoice should be numbered (number one is the earliest date), but kept in invoice date order. The number should be entered in the voucher number column in the analysis book when an invoice is paid by cheque.

4. Managing cash

This is the hardest area to manage. It is the one subject that causes difficulty, both in record-keeping and in accountability to the tax authorities.

If you use an accountant, they will probably ask you to keep a cash book to help them understand what has happened. As you are probably not an accountant yourself, I anticipate that you may find the principles of the cash book quite hard to follow. I would therefore not bother (I hope I can maintain relationships with accountants after saying this!). If you do your own accounts, you certainly do not need a formal cash book.

What you **will** need to do is keep a record of cash coming in to the business and cash payments made by it. This can be done at the time a cash transaction occurs, using the simple filing system explained in this section earlier.

Cash given to you
Normally, this will be in the form of fees from clients. These should be paid into the TC bank account with the client invoice number listed on the bank paying in slip, and payment noted on the invoice in your lever arch file.

Left hand page of Analysis Book:
MONEY PAID INTO BANK

Your Income

Date 2003	Received from	Voucher No./Fee invoice	Total	VAT	Cheques for fees	Cash for fees	Total fees	Other	Deduct from expenses
Apr 6	Client A	001	60.00			60.00	60.00		
6	Client B	002	25.00		25.00		25.00		
8	Client C	003	300.00		300.00		300.00		
9	Authors Fees	Pay in slip 01	186.25		186.25		186.25		
10	Client D	004	150.00		150.00		150.00		
11	Transfer from deposit A/C	/	2000.00					2000.00	
12	Client E	005	20.00			20.00	20.00		
13	Insurance rebate	Pay in slip 02	10.21						10.21
15	Client F	006	100.00			100.00	100.00		
17	Client G	007	50.00		50.00		50.00		
21	Conference fee (speaker)	Pay in slip 03	350.00		350.00		350.00		
24	Bank interest on deposit A/C	/	29.56				29.56		
27	Client H	008	35.00			35.00	35.00		
	TOTAL FOR APRIL		3316.02				1305.81		10.21

Right hand page of Analysis Book:: MONEY PAID OUT OF BANK

Your Income ← | Add these columns to get total expenses → | These items not Tax deductible →

Date 2003	Paid to	Voucher	Total	VAT	Drawings for self	Room Hire	Printing Stationery Postage	Bank Charges	Hotel Travel Car	Books Journals	Fees Insurance	Other expenses	Other payments
Apr 6	Room Hire Ltd	001	94.00	14.00		80.00							
6	Insurance	002	117.50								117.50		
8	Car expenses - self	003	220.00						220.00				
8	Stationery Ltd	004	23.50	3.50			20.00						
9	Cashed cheque	PCT 1*	100.00										100.00
9	National Insurance Class 2	/	8.67										8.67
10	Credit Card	005	117.50	17.50			20.00		80.00				
11	Website Co Ltd	006	352.50	52.50								Advertising 300.00	
12	Petty Cash Cheque	PCT 2*	75.00	5.32		40.00	29.78						
12	Client B bounced cheque	/	25.00									bad debt 25.00	
13	Inland Revenue tax paid	/	1100.60										1100.60
15	AZ computers	007	117.50	117.50								computer 1000.00	
16	Conference costs	008	235.00	35.00							200.00		
18	Local Bookshop	009	24.99							24.99			
19	Bank charges	/	8.00					8.00					
30	Bank interests	/	10.14					10.14					
30	Cheque to self	/	1500.00		1500.00								
	TOTAL FOR APRIL		3,629.90			120.00	69.78	18.14	300.00	24.99	317.50	1325.00	

CHECK YOUR BANK STATEMENTS LIKE THIS:
• Money in bank at 5th April PLUS total money paid into bank LESS total money paid out of bank EQUALS money in bank at 30th April

* see page 26

If, for some reason, you need this cash personally before banking it, pay your business account a personal cheque for the same amount, list the client invoices on the paying-in slip as before, and again enter the payment detail in the lever arch file. Do this immediately, otherwise confusion will quickly reign!

Expenses paid by you in cash
If you have to pay expenses in cash the best way to do this is to use a petty cash tin (PCT). Start by cashing a business cheque for a petty cash float - £100 should be enough. Enter this business cheque on the right hand side of the analysis book, and under voucher number, put PCT-1. Put your receipts for cash expenditure into the cash tin. When the money starts to run out in the tin, add up the value of all the receipts for expenditure in the tin. Put the total clearly on the top receipt, clip them together, mark them PCT-2, and file them in the lever arch file at the top of your expenditure invoices. Cash a TC business account cheque for exactly the same amount, and enter the cheque on the right hand side of the analysis book. The voucher number in the analysis book should say PCT-2 and will be the same number as you have in your invoice file. Follow this procedure whenever the cash in the tin starts to run out (continuing with PCT-3, PCT-4 etc. for each bundle of receipts). Always file petty cash receipts for expenses at the top of your invoices in the lever arch file, so that you can easily add them up at the end of the year. (Remember any VAT you have been charged is non-claimable).

Following these rules will help you avoid any problems at the end of the year.

5. Working out your profit or loss at year-end.

Your profit or net income is calculated like this:

> Income from fees **(A)** **less** Allowable expenses **(B)**
> = Net income (or profit)

A. *Income*

1 **Add up** all the fees and disbursements you have received for this tax year (6th April to 5th April) using the **paying-in side of the analysis book**
2 **Deduct** any fees you received at the beginning of the tax year which relate to your **invoices dated in the previous tax year**.
3 **Add** any fees that have been invoiced but **not yet been paid for** in this tax year.

> The result is your total income for this tax year = A

B. *Expenses*

1 **Add up** all the expense invoices, including the petty cash receipts at the front, which you have entered into the lever arch file dated within this tax year. Make sure you turn out your pockets/hand bags/wallets and have them all entered! Remember to subtract the VAT. Check the total with the entries you have made in the analysis book in the expense column.
2 **Add** the value of any expense receipts still in the petty cash tin dated in this tax year (minus VAT).

> The result is your total expenses for the tax year = B

> **A - B =** Net income or profit for the year

This figure will now form the basis for calculating your tax and National Insurance payments. Please note that the question of whether invoices have been paid or not is not relevant to working out your net income.

You will, however, need to keep a close eye on money due to you that has not been paid on time. That is why I recommend that each year, when you calculate your income, you follow the procedure I outline, rather than simply adding up the copy fee invoices in your lever arch file. By referring to the analysis book you will see who has not paid you at the end of the year. You can also, if you wish, compare the analysis book with the lever arch file as a final check.

On the expenses side I have recommended adding up the invoices and petty cash receipts in your lever arch file. This is because you can leave it to the people to whom you owe money to chase you themselves! You will need the paid out side of the analysis book to check if you have already paid bills for which you are being chased. Make sure you have recorded all your expenditure within the tax year, whether invoiced or not, as it is tax deductible.

An example of how an income and expenditure should look is shown in **Appendix** I. This form can also be attached to your tax return as it stands.

YOUR MINIMUM PAPERWORK - CHECKLIST

✓ Tick when you have:

☐ Analysis book - e.g. Collins Cathedral Analysis Book
                    Number 150/12.1

☐ Bank statement file

☐ Chequebook stubs

☐ Paying-in slips

☐ Box file for keeping cheque book stubs and paying-in slips

☐ Lever-arch file for filing invoices raised by you and invoices received by you plus petty cash expenses

☐ Petty cash tin

Section D
EXPENSES

I. Basic principles

I have talked to a number of therapists who have had disagreements with the Inland Revenue over what constitutes an allowable expense for the business (and therefore tax deductible). Contrary to popular folklore, the Inland Revenue staff are usually helpful, reasonable, sensible and logical - once you manage to get through to them.

The fundamental principle regarding allowable expenses for therapists and counsellors is that:-

Expenses incurred should be wholly and exclusively for the operation and development of the business

EXAMPLE
Sally, a play therapist, wanted to claim a pair of new jeans as an allowable tax deductible expense for her sandplay work with children. The Inland Revenue refused, as the jeans could and would be worn by Sally for other uses.

Mia, a dramatherapist, wanted to claim a full-length apron for her finger-painting work with children. The Inland Revenue accepted this claim, as the garment would not be worn for any other purpose.

The example demonstrates that there can be quite a fine line between allowable and not allowable expenditure. Reference to the exact wording of the rule above should help you decide.

**The following business expenses should be tax deductible –
use these as a check list:**

- Accountant's fees
- Advertising and promotion of the business
- Books and journals
- Business bank charges and interest on overdraft (interest on savings is taxable)
- Business postage
- Business stationery
- Business telephone costs
- Computer for maintaining records
- Continuous professional development courses (some provisos)
- Course fees
- Employee costs
- Furniture for business use
- Legal advice in relation to professional issues
- Professional insurance
- Room Hire (but see detail on using the home as an office)
- Special tools and equipment for use for and with clients
- Subscriptions to journals or professional associations in your field
- Supervision costs
- Therapy or counselling (if this is a compulsory requirement of a course leading to professional qualification)
- Travel costs from work to client or training (but not from home to work)

It is also possible to claim for relevant expenses incurred in the past. This is important, because items such as fees for courses leading to professional qualification, and the costs of therapy and supervision required by that course, are, by definition, past expenses. (See also Section G – Offsetting past losses).

You must have supporting documentation for all expenses claimed – ask for and keep receipts for everything you spend on items in the list above.

2. Consulting Rooms

Therapists and counsellors generally either hire rooms or work from a separate room at home. If you hire rooms, make sure you obtain an invoice from the landlord, or at the very least, a receipt for your payment. Claiming these costs as an expense should be straightforward.

Working from home raises a complex issue from the tax angle. Generally, the Inland Revenue will accept an annual expense charge for 'use of home as office'. This charge can encompass electricity, telephone (land line, mobile, fax and Internet), gas and small essential items of furniture and equipment. You can charge a proportion of house insurance, based on the area of the house used in business. A typical charge for all items would not normally exceed £800 in a tax year.

If you attempt to charge more than this, say by way of a commercial rent (- for example, £10 per square foot per annum for a 180 square foot room – £1,800 per annum, plus council tax based on the proportion the room is of the total house or flat area), you run the very considerable risk of paying capital gains tax on that part of the house or flat you have used as business premises if you sell the property. If you operate from a one bedroom flat, this is clearly a serious matter. The Capital Gain is crystallised when you sell your flat or house, and tax will likely be between 22% and 40% of the gain after your annual tax-free allowance for Capital Gain of £7,900 (2003/2004) is used up. The tax is calculated on how long you have used part of the premises for commercial use, and what proportion of the house or flat has been used for this purpose.

That being said, however, you can of course set up a dedicated telephone/fax line for the business, and charge the whole expense of it.

3. Course Fees

Course fees (and the costs of therapy and supervision undertaken

as course requirements) are tax deductible, if they relate to your qualification and practice as a therapist or counsellor. They should be claimed immediately you commence business (subject to the provisos detailed in Section G – Offsetting past losses) . Therapists and counsellors already in business can claim against next year's profits.

You can also claim some ongoing professional training. The training that your governing body, such as the BACP (British Association of Counsellors and Psychotherapists), considers essential to remain accredited, is tax deductible. Further, any specific training to address ongoing specific and related client issues is claimable. Likewise conferences, training days and workshops that address specific client needs are claimable. Courses and conferences that add to your general knowledge and understanding may not be tax deductible. The guiding principle is - **is it wholly and exclusively for the operation of the business?** If you have a client with ADHD, for example, a conference on this issue would be deductible; whereas one on, say, 'difficult people' might not be. This is sometimes an imprecise area, and you are often going to need to rely on the interpretation of your local tax inspector as to what constitutes 'wholly and exclusively'.

Psychotherapy and counselling books are tax deductible. Journals and professional subscriptions, including professional insurance, are too.

4. Travel Costs

You can only claim travel expenses from **place of work to client**, not from home to workplace. If you work at home, you can claim from home to client.

If you are using your own car to travel, the most tax efficient (and easiest) way to claim is to charge the business 40 pence a mile. This is tax free to you personally up to 10,000 miles a year at 40 pence (20 pence a mile over that). The charge can also be used by the business as a tax-deductible item. You will need to back up your mileage claim with journey details (destinations and distances) and dates.

If your work requires an overnight stay, you can claim an evening meal in addition to normal bed & breakfast expenses. Expenditure on entertainment and most gifts is not tax-deductible.

Can I claim expenses incurred in previous years?

If you have forgotten to claim an expense, even a major one like course fees, you can still claim this expense in the current tax year **providing** you have retained or can obtain the invoice or relevant paperwork justifying the expense.

5. Claiming expenses as an employee

Some therapists and counsellors may work only for one single agency or Company (for example, an agency which offers counselling within employee assistance programmes). In these circumstances you are not self-employed; rather, **you are considered an employee of the agency or Company as far as tax matters are concerned**. This is true, irrespective of whether you are on the employer's PAYE system, or whether you send your employer your invoice for fees. Being an employee means that you normally would not be able to claim expenses against tax.

If your employer reimburses your expenses

From the 6th April 2003, contributions to using the home as an office and travel costs paid by an employer are tax free up to £104 in a tax year, and higher than this, if an employer can provide **supporting evidence** that any additional expenses they reimburse to you are needed to fulfil your commitment to them. Previously, such expenses paid by an employer would have been treated as taxable income.

If you incur expense and your employer does not reimburse you
There are certain types of expenditure which, if wholly and exclusively necessary for your job and paid for by you, may be claimed against your income. To help your claim it is worthwhile obtaining a letter from your employer confirming that, while your expenses are justified and necessary for your job, they are not reimbursed as a matter of policy.

The expenses you may be able to claim under this heading are: use of your own car for business (providing it is used to visit different places regularly), telephone calls to clients, books and journals, essential professional fees including insurance and supervision. Under certain circumstances you might also be able to claim a charge for using your home as an office if you see agency clients there. If you use a separate room at home exclusively for clients, you can charge a proportion of the cost that the room represents of all household costs. If you do this, the expense should be entered in the 'other expenses' box in the Employment sheet on your tax return. Please remember also that there may be a capital gain to pay when you sell your house or flat if you charge out your consulting room in this way (*see sub-section 2 above*).

If you are a healthcare worker
A set of flat-rate expenses was introduced in tax year 1998-1999. Your tax office will consider claims for the five years prior to the current tax year if you have not claimed expenses to which you were entitled.

NATIONAL INSURANCE

I. Basic Principles

As a self-employed person you are responsible for paying your own National Insurance Contributions.

Being self-employed affects:

- The social security benefits you can claim, such as unemployment benefit
- Other rights, for example those under employment legislation, such as the right to maternity leave, or to a redundancy payment, notice rights and so on
- Your liability to the public for the work you do for them

The first two points are modified by individual circumstances and fall outside the remit of this book. The last point on public liability will be covered by your professional insurance, which you must have by law.

Self-employed National Insurance rates are different from those you pay as an employee. The purpose of the payments remains the same; it is to preserve your social security and pension rights.

Self-employed therapists and counsellors pay two rates:

- *Class 2 contributions*
  These are paid every thirteen weeks. You are excused the payment of these if your net income is less than £4,095 for tax year 2003/2004. A Class 2 contribution is £2 per week, maximum £104 per annum. It can be paid by monthly direct debit. It can be paid

from your business account, but it is not tax deductible as an expense item.

■ Class 4 contributions

These are paid yearly when you submit your tax return. Class 4 contributions are based on your final profit or net income for the tax year, and are calculated for tax year 2003/2004 as follows:

Profits up to £4,615	**NIL**
Profits £4615-£30,940	**8% of profit**
Profits over £30,940	**1% of excess profit**

Class 4 contributions of necessity are paid at the time you submit your tax return. They can be paid by the TC business account, but **are also not income tax deductible**.

If you are employed AND self-employed

If you are employed and self-employed, and pay more than the prescribed amount of National Insurance Contributions for a tax year, you may be able to get a refund. You should apply for a refund if you pay more than -

- £2,628.80 in Class 1, Class 2 and Class 4 National Insurance Contributions in the 2002/2003 tax year. A refund will only be made if it is more than £3. (Class 1 contributions are only paid if you are an employee)

or
- £1,912.35 in Class 2 and Class 4 National Insurance Contributions in the 2002/2003 tax year.

In these circumstances, you can get a refund of the Class 4 National Insurance Contributions. These maximum limits were abolished from 6th April 2003, and will therefore only apply to National Insurance paid in the financial year ending 5th April 2003.

PERSONAL PENSIONS

I. Basic principles

Your National Insurance contributions entitle you to the state pension on retirement. **You may wish to add to that pension with additional savings**. This can be in the form of a personal pension or simply through a savings scheme you devise yourself. The government has encouraged people recently to invest more in private pensions, largely to reduce the burden on the state of supporting an ageing population. The encouragement takes the form of tax incentives. These incentives are important for the therapists or counsellors to appraise.

A pension is simply an investment. It is subject to the same market forces as all other investments - its value may go up, or it may go down. Recently it has gone down for most people, leaving many to reconsider the virtues of pensions compared to other forms of investment.

2. Personal pensions for the self-employed therapist or counsellor

Pension contributions are paid before income tax is deducted. There are rules as to how much a self-employed therapist or counsellor can contribute to a pension from profits (see Table below). You are allowed to contribute a substantial amount each year. For example, if you are aged between 51 and 55 at the beginning of the tax year, and you have earned £40,000 net income in that year, you can contribute 30% of that (£12,000) to a pension fund **free of tax**. You are also allowed to go back 12 months and add to the previous year's pension contribution, providing the total for that year does not exceed the allowable amount for that year (see Table below again). If you do this, any extra contribution must be organised and paid for before the end of ten months after the last tax year (in other words, by 31st January). This is particularly useful if you have just had a good year for income.

Maximum tax free pension contribution limits for self-employed therapists and consellors	
Age at beginning of tax year	Percentage of income allowed for Personal Pension Plan
up to 35	17.5
36 - 45	20
46 - 50	25
51 - 55	30
56 - 60	35
61 and over	40

Note: The maximum earnings figure from which tax free contributions can be deducted is £99,000 for the tax year 2003/4

You will need to get professional advice (from an accountant) initially, regarding setting up and contributing to a personal pension. When you reach statutory retirement age (60 for women and 65 for men) you can 'draw down' (access) your pension. You can only access, as a lump sum payment, 25% of the 'pot' of money your contributions have created, although this payment is tax-free. Your regular pension income comes from the remainder of the 'pot' and is taxable. **For the self-employed therapist or counsellor, there are clearly substantial tax benefits attached to pension contributions.**

The problem with pension contributions alone as a form of saving and investment for the future is that you lock away a lot of money until you retire (when you may need some of it beforehand). To many people, this is a perfectly acceptable position, but it might not suit everyone. The only alternative to a pension plan is **straightforward investment made from after tax income.**

Once you have decided how much money a year you would like to put aside in the form of a pension, it may be sensible to consider **personal savings** as well as pension contributions. Personal savings can be put into long-term interest-bearing savings accounts with banks and building societies, but have the advantage that there are no rules attached to the investment. Money can be withdrawn at any time in your life. The disadvantage is that personal savings have to come from *after* tax income, whereas pension contributions come *before* taxed income.

Section G
INCOME TAX

1. Basic principles

Although you are a therapy and counselling business, you do not pay tax at corporation tax rates as companies do. **You pay income tax on your profits**. You can therefore claim your personal allowances and benefits before paying tax on your income less expenses. You also pay your income tax using the same tax bands as you would as a personal taxpayer.

If you are employed as well as running a therapy and counselling business, you can still easily complete the tax form. You will use the information on your Form P60 given to you annually by your employer or your Form P45, but you can also attach your business accounts at the back of the tax return. The income from your business will be added to any taxable income you have received as an employee and taxed in total accordingly. You can see an example in **Appendix 2**.

For the first year in business, you must pay the income tax you have calculated you owe between 6th April and 31st January, for the first tax year ended 5th April previous.

EXAMPLE
Grace started work as a counsellor in October 2002. She has to pay her tax year 2002/2003 bill by 31st January 2004.

You then have to make an interim payment for the next tax year by 31st July that year. This interim payment should be **half of the total payment you made in the previous year** unless your circumstances have changed dramatically. If they have changed, a note to the Inland Revenue explaining the changes and the reason for your interim payment will suffice. You then pay the balance of that tax year by 31st January, and so on.

EXAMPLE
Reiko was due to pay tax of £1,000 for her first tax year in business - 2002/2003. She paid £1,000 during January 2004, and a further £500 (half the 2002/2003 figure) as an interim payment for tax year 2003/2004 during July 2004. Eventually she finds that her tax bill was £1,200 for tax year 2003/2004 so she pays the balance she owes for that year of £700 (£1,200 - £500 already paid) during January 2005.

It is better, if you can, to complete and submit your return together with a payment by 30th September. This will give you time to amend your calculations if you have underpaid and, conversely, if you are owed money by the Inland Revenue, you will obtain it quicker. If you wish, you can now submit your return electronically on the Internet.

The income tax is payable on net income, that is, **income after deducting allowable expenses**. The correct way to display these figures to the Inland Revenue is by using an Income and Expenditure Account for the year 6th April to 5th April (see **Appendix 1**).

2. Profit level and tax payable

Each individual under the age of 65, for the tax year 2003/2004, has an **individual allowance of £4,615**. This can be deducted from profit before any tax is payable.

The 2003/2004 income tax rates on the remainder of your profit are:
- First   £1,960   10% income tax =   £196 maximum
- Next   £28,540   22% income tax = £6,279 maximum
- Over   £30,500   40% income tax on the excess only

EXAMPLE

Keith earned £25,000 this tax year (2003/2004) from Social Services before tax. He also runs a TC business, which made a profit of £17,000 in this same tax year. His tax bill was:

		Tax payable
• Personal allowance	£4,615	£0
• First	£1,960	£196
• Next	£28,540	£6,279
• Next	£6,885	£ 2,754
Total	**£42,000**	**£9,229**

*(The Social Services Department for which Keith works will have already deducted tax and national insurance – see **Appendix 2**.)*

3. Offsetting past losses against income

As a TC business, you could make a loss rather than a profit in any tax year. This happens when your expenditure exceeds your income. When you first start in business, it is possible that you will incur a **trading loss** in the first year. This may well be because you decide to claim past course fees in this period.

As I wrote earlier, many therapist or counsellors do not realise that the considerable sums of money you have spent to become qualified can be offset against income **once you are self-employed**. The following rules apply to trading losses.

If you make a loss in your business, and you are also an employee or have other income, you can deduct the loss from -

- this income and then capital gains tax (if any) if all events occur in the same tax year.
- other income and then capital gains tax (if any) of the previous year

- trading profits of future years
- any income in the preceding three tax years, **subject to** the loss arising in the first four tax years of the business. Losses are set against the earliest trading years first.
- any profits over the previous tax years if the loss arises in the last twelve months before closing down.

For therapists and counsellors, the importance of these rules lies in the way course fees in particular are claimed against business income. Course fees can be many thousands of pounds and claiming them can therefore help you save a lot of tax, particularly in the early years of your business.

However, you need to be careful how you claim for the fees. You must claim the whole of the loss before any other tax relief. Therefore, before making a claim, you should calculate whether you would lose a significant proportion of your personal allowances and deductions. If, after deducting the loss, you find that the remaining income is insufficient to cover your personal allowances, it may be better to **carry forward the whole loss with a view to setting it off against future profits** from your business in another tax year. Please think this through carefully, as a lot of your money is involved.

EXAMPLE
Roger made a loss of £3,500 in his first tax year as a therapist. In the same tax year, he received £4,500 income from his savings. Roger has a tax free personal allowance of £4,615. He will not pay tax on his savings income, because his personal allowance is greater than this income. Roger therefore decides to carry forward his tax loss made as a therapist this year to next year, when he expects his total income to be well in excess of his personal allowance.

If you wish to do this, it is worthwhile consulting an accountant.

4. Capital Allowances that reduce your tax bill

Currently, it is possible for TC businesses to claim **100% of the cost of a new computer and related software** against income tax in the tax year in which it was purchased. This tax concession lasts until 31st March 2004. Normally, major items of expense such as this can only be claimed against tax over a period of years.

From 17th April 2002, it has also been possible to claim the complete cost (excluding VAT) of a small car whose exhaust carbon dioxide emissions are 120gm/km or less (the car dealer will tell you which cars these are!) against income in one year. If you need to use a car a lot for your business, this might be attractive. Private use of this car is a benefit to you, however, and you will have to pay tax on this benefit. The amount of tax you pay depends on what sort of car it is, what fuel it uses, how old it is and how many business miles you do in it. If you do not use an accountant, you will need to check the information on the Inland Revenue website or read the appropriate leaflet (*see* Useful Information).

And finally.......

Money isn't everything; it usually isn't even enough! **Anon**

It's OK! It's OK to think about rewarding yourself with a good living. After all, you have spent a long time and a lot of money acquiring the knowledge and expertise essential for your work. Your contribution to the lives of your clients will be invaluable to them and, as a professional, it is perfectly reasonable to charge appropriate professional fees. Your clients are consumers like the rest of us, and are used to dealing with money. They will not be surprised to have to talk about money at the appropriate moments.

I hope that you have found this book useful, clear and, at times, even enlightening. Above all, I hope it will enhance your own financial return.

Money matters can be handled quickly and efficiently. Paperwork can be kept to a minimum, as can your tax bill. Just a few minutes a month spent on money will free you to focus on what really matters most to you - working with your clients. Good luck.

Appendix I

An example of an Income and Expenditure Account.

TC BUSINESS ACCOUNT - INCOME AND EXPENDITURE
6th April 2003 to 5th April 2004

Income

	£
Client Fees and Disbursements	22,400
Interest received on Deposit Account	162
Total Income	**22,562**

Less

Expenses (excluding VAT):

Room Hire	600
Course Fees	3,100
Supervision costs	1,200
Conference Fees (CPD)	280
Books and journals	328
Advertising and promotion	341
Legal advice	300
Professional Insurance	120
New Computer (100% capital allowance)	1,020
Proportion of 'home as office'	630
Stationery and postage	310
Car Expenses	600
Bank charges	175
Subscriptions	80
Hotel costs	124

Total Expenditure	**- 9,208**
Net Income (or profit)*	**13,354**

*This is the figure on which income tax is based. It is also the figure (if you are self-employed only) on which you calculate the maximum allowable personal pension contribution and your class 4 National Insurance Contribution.

Appendix 2
An example of a tax calculation where the therapist or counsellor is both employed and in business as a self-employed person

TAX COMPUTATION - YEAR ENDING 5th APRIL 2004
FOR: A THERAPIST/COUNSELLOR

	Amount £	Tax Paid £
Income from employment		
A Tutor at XYZ College - P60 or P45 pay	8,250	1,865.20
Income from Self-Employment		
B Total taxable net income (Appendix 1)	13,354	
Tax Return Entries		
UK personal account bank interest - 20% tax deducted at source		46.00
Personal Pension - relief claimed (see Note 1)	3,354	
Total Net Relevant Earnings (A+B)*	**21,604**	

■ Tax calculation on net relevant earnings

Income	
Employment	8,250
Self-Employment	13,354
Total Income	21,604
Less reliefs claimed	- 3,354
Statutory total income	18,250
Less Personal Allowance	- 4,615
Net Taxable Income	**13,635**

■ Tax bands and amounts payable

	Amount £	Tax £
10% on	1,960	196.00
22% on	11,675	2568.50
40% on	0	0.00
	13,635	
Add relief at source on pension contribution (Note 1)		737.88
Total tax assessed		3502.38

Tax paid

Employment	1,865.20	
Savings	46.00	
Less total tax paid		- 1911.20
Tax Outstanding (C)		1591.18

■ National Insurance Contributions

Class 4 Contributions:			
	First	4,615	0.00
	Next	8,739	699.12
		13,354	
Total tax (C) and National Insurance due			**2290.30**

* Net relevant earnings is the income figure on which you can calculate your maximum allowable personal pension contributions

Note 1. Since the 6th April 2001, all contributions to personal pension plans are payable net of basic rate (currently 22%) tax.

USEFUL INFORMATION

A. Inland Revenue

■ HELPLINES:

National Insurance:

Self-Employed Helpline
Telephone: 0845 915 4655
Open 8am to 5pm Monday to Friday

National Insurance Contributions Office
(Switchboard) **Telephone:** 0191 213 5000
Open 8am to 5.30pm Monday to Friday

Income Tax:

Newly Self-Employed Helpline
Telephone: 08459 15 45 15
Open 8am to 8pm seven days a week

Self Assessment Helpline
Telephone: 0845 9000 444
Open 8am to 8pm seven days a week

Self Assessment Orderline for extra
information, leaflets, etc
Telephone: 0845 9000 404
Open 8am to 10pm seven days a week
Fax: 0845 9000 604
Email: saorderline.in@gtnet.gov.uk
Address: P.O. Box 37, St. Austell, PL25 5YN

■ LEAFLETS

The following Inland Revenue Booklets are particularly helpful for the self-employed

IR56	Employed or Self Employed?
PSE1	Thinking of working for yourself?
CWF1	Notification of becoming self employed.
SA/BK8	Self Assessment. Your Guide.
SA/BK3	Self Assessment. A guide to keeping records for the Self Employed.
CA02	Self Employed people with small earnings 2003/2004
CWL2	National Insurance Contributions for Self Employed People. Class 2 and Class 4 contributions.
IR78	Personal Pensions - A guide for tax

■ WEBSITE

The Inland Revenue website is **www.inlandrevenue.gov.uk**. You can access all the booklets above on this website. You will need Adobe Acrobat Reader to download certain files, but not the ones above.

B. Banks and how they can help

Most people will bank with one of the four major high street banks (Royal Bank of Scotland/NatWest, Lloyds/TSB, Barclays and HSBC). All of these banks recommend that you talk to your local manager who will direct you to the local small business manager. All of the banks claim they are supportive of small businesses. The bank that appears to obtain the best service awards for small business is HSBC.

All of these banks operate a website. Do look at these if you can. They are:

RBS/NatWest   **www.natwest.com**

Lloyds/TSB   **www.success4business.com**

Barclays   **www.business.barclays.co.uk**

HSBC   **www.ukbusiness.hsbc.com**

Both Lloyds and Barclays appear to want you to disclose who you are before offering information. If you do not want to do this, use HSBC or RBS/NatWest.

In addition to these banks, Alliance and Leicester have a very helpful website: **www.alliancebusinessbanking.co.uk**

The range of services provided by all these banks is comprehensive and will cover all your needs.

The major banks offer Internet banking and details can be found on their Websites.

Examples of savings for the next edition of MONEY MATTERS

The publishers would be happy to hear from anyone who is able to give an example of a personal saving they have made through using the information in this book, especially if the example will help other therapists and counsellors make similar savings when the book is updated.

Please contact Andrea at Worth Publishing on 020 7266 0333 or by e-mail: andrea@worthpublishing.demon.co.uk